Copyright © 2020 Michelle Anderson

All rights reserved

Published by No Flocks Publishing 2020

Edition No.1

Ring a Ring a Rosé

For tired mums,
you need it.

For Blake and Zak,
my favourite Goofy Goobers.
I love you more than Milka.

And to PA,
love of my life,
For showing my boys the right way
to treat a girl.

Life isn't about waiting for the storm to pass. It's learning to dance in the rain.
- Anonymous -

A Message from Michelle.

Mum guilt is the worst kind of guilt. We should read to our kids and we want to read to them, but it's a drag when after book twenty-eight instead of being sleepy, they start acting as if they've just downed a double shot macchiato. I wrote this book for you, the tired mum who could do with a wine.

No matter how much you *think* you know about parenting from reading books, observing other mums, Googling or even being an aunt, when you become a mother it's a total slap in the face. There are no instructions and no one really knows what they're doing. If there's a mum you know and you're envious because she has it all together, she hasn't. She's honestly just like you and me and has no idea what she's going to do next, but she knows how to look like she has it together. And remember, you are most likely that mum to someone else. We are ALL rolling the dice and hoping for the best. After all, our job is to give our kids enough stories to make them interesting, and just enough trauma to make them funny, right?

Before children, our social lives used to be planning an event outfit, shopping alone for it, creating a Pinterest board for new hair ideas and picking out the perfect palette for our makeup... now we're down to rare night out where we have a quick shower neck down, our hair in a mum bun and do our makeup one-handed while a kid sits on our lap getting into our favourite lip kit. If we are honest, our perfect night now involves going to the toilet alone and several hours of unbroken sleep.

My best advice is to find some mum friends who want to talk about poo and pee and vomit and who's had the least sleep because well, this is your life now.

Please don't lose your mind worrying about reference to mums' drinking in this book. We can have a drink! Actually, it's less about drinking and more about daydreaming about drinking, about taking time for yourself because you need it. Truth is, I don't think I had a drink for at least two years after my first born, but I *thought* a lot about having a drink. I was just too tired to bother. We all love our kids but we can't help that sometimes our minds wander back to the days where we were childless, young and free, and there's nothing wrong with that.

If you like, take some advice from your children, and use your imagination. I found even drinking sparkling water from a nice fancy glass while cooking dinner can take the edge off. It's called a Mumjito (Mum-he-tow). Take your fancy glass, muddled lime*, ice, sparkling water, clapped mint** and when necessary – add vodka.

When your kids go off to school you are not known by your name anymore, you're just [insert your kid's name here]'s Mum. However, I have found it's really important to still be you sometimes too. Find a way to have regular grown-up only time; it does wonders for you. If you have a partner, date night is amazing, - even if all you can do is put the kids to bed early and put some lippy on while wearing your PJs. As good (or better), go and have a girl's night out! You will miss the kids; they will miss you. You'll arrive home recharged, which means you'll be a better parent, which means you'll have happy kids.

When everything was crazy, I used to put the music up loud (to drown out any whinging) and have dance parties in the lounge room with the kids and just let loose. They don't care what you look like dancing – they just love you having fun with them. You might sound like a dying goat rather than Beyoncé and Dad might dance more like Mr. Bean than Channing Tatum but it doesn't matter. They won't judge you. It'll be years before you get embarrassing. Have fun and enjoy it while you can.

This book was created for you to read and sing to your little ones, who will love you spending the time with them, and allow to you have a little smirk at the reality of parenthood while loving it all the same.

Above all, love them, love the sh%& out of them, because they really do grow up before your eyes.

Good luck and have fun.
With love,
Michelle

*muddled lime – fancy way of saying squeeze it by squashing it with a wooden spoon in the cup.
**clapped mint – in craft cocktail bars they literally take fresh mint and throw it up in the air and clap it in their hands to release the oils and bring out the flavour.

Table of Contents

1. Baa Baa Bar Man.

2. Twinkle, Twinkle.

3. The Little Teapot.

4. Once I Caught a Fish Alive.

5. Three Tired Mums.

6. You Are Tired & You Know It.

7. Ring a Ring a Rosé.

Baa Baa Bar Man.
Sung to the tune of Baa Baa Black Sheep.

Baa baa bar man, have you any wine?

Yes sir, yes sir, all the time.

One for my wife please, she'll have the new rosé

Date night comes just once a month,

we live for this day.

Twinkle, Twinkle.

Sung to the tune of Twinkle, Twinkle, Little Star.

Twinkle, twinkle, little star,

take me to the closest bar.

Cocktails on a roof top high,

Mummy needs a big Mai Tai.

A Fruit Tingle, then shots all round.

Dancing 'til we're homeward bound.

The little Teapot.
Sung to the tune of I'm a little Teapot.

Vodka in my teapot, yes it's true.

I've cleaned up the vomit and I've cleaned up the poo.

When I finished cleaning I found you,

drinking water from the loo.

Once I Caught a Fish Alive.

Sung to the tune of the same name.

1, 2, 3, 4, 5, Daddy caught a fish alive.

6, 7, 8, 9, 10, then he let it go again.

Why can't he fish no more?

Because he can't get out the door.

When can he go again?

When Mummy gets some sleep that's when!

Three Tired Mums.

 *Sung to the tune of Three Blind Mice.*

Three tired mums, three tired mums.

None of them can run, none of them can run.

They haven't slept in quite a time.

They push to the front of the coffee line.

Hurry up or they'll have to have wine.

They're three tired mums.

You Are Tired & You Know it.

♫ Sung to the tune of If You're Happy & You Know It.

If you're tired and you know it, have a drink.
For years and years you haven't slept a wink.
When you're feelin' quite defeated, all your patience is depleted.
Put the kids to bed and go and pour a drink.

When you watch them sleep it really makes you think.
Even though they nearly drive you to the brink.
When they smile then there's no doubt, this is just what life's about.
Take your time and just be careful not to blink.

Ring a Ring a Rosé.

Sung to the tune of Ring a Ring a Rosie.

Ring a ring a rosé.

We've had a really good day.

I kiss you. I kiss you.

We all lay down!

(And go to sleep, goodnight!)

Recipe for Mumjito
(Mum-he-tow)

Take a fancy glass.

Quarter fresh limes and muddle in.

Add ice and fresh mint

(make sure you 'clap' the mint).

Fill with sparkling water.

Add vodka when necessary.

And now CHEERS to the best job in the world!

About the Author

Michelle Anderstarr is a professional mum with over twenty-two years' experience, having successfully raised her kids to be pretty awesome adults. She lives in her Little Blue House in North Queensland, Australia, with her husband Paul, and fur babies, Koda the dog and Princess Leia the cat. Michelle has two grown up boys, Blake and Zak, and two step-children, Safiyah and Maalik. She brought the boys up as a young single mum and was *that mum* riding on the BMX track and up in the playground with them. They grew up watching *The SpongeBob SquarePants Movie* every Sunday, and they sat down for dinner together every night at 6pm when *The Simpsons* came on. This book is a celebration of getting them to adulthood.

Follow her journey on her author website at
www.MichelleAnderstarr.com

And find out what other exciting adventures Flocker the Flamingo is up to on Instagram @ringaringa_rose_aye and Facebook @RingaRingaRosé.

#ringaringarosé